Psalms That Touch Us Where We Live

David R. Mains

David C. Cook Publishing Co.

ELGIN, ILLINOIS—WESTON, ONTARIO

T5-CVH-119

Published by David C. Cook Publishing Co., Elgin, IL 60120
Cover design by Joe Ragont
Printed in the United States of America
ISBN 0-89191-265-7
LC 80-51283

CONTENTS

The Chapel Talks Series
by David Mains

Making Church More Enjoyable
How to Support Your Pastor
How to Resist Temptation
God, Help Us with the Kids
What's Wrong with Lukewarm?
Praying More Effectively
Getting to Know the Holy Spirit
When God Gets Angry with a Nation
A Closer Walk with God
Psalms That Touch Us Where We Live
Making Scripture Yours
I Needed That Encouragement

INTRODUCTION

Most people listen to the radio while they're doing something else. As a broadcaster I'm aware that a person hearing me is probably shaving, fixing breakfast, driving to work, or some similar activity. Being able to keep his or her attention in such a setting is a lot different than preaching to a captive audience.

Therefore, I was dubious as to whether the slow pace of radio with its need for frequent repetition and underscoring each key truth would transfer all that well into print.

To complicate matters further, every time a program is made I must assume many listeners didn't hear what was said the day before. But just the opposite is true when compiling the chapters of a book. They build on one another.

Well, the first series of Chapel talks is now completed. Through the help of others, my broadcast scripts have been made more readable than I thought possible. The greatest thanks for this project goes to my wife, Karen, who put aside her own writing to help me out. Two Chapel of the Air staff members, Ruby Christian and Sharon Morse, also did yeoman duty typing long hours after work and on weekends.

1

THE DIGNITY OF MAN:
Psalm 8

When I was pastor of a church in Chicago, I would occasionally visit the Reverend Jesse Jackson's Saturday Operation PUSH rally. A traditional part of those early morning meetings was a chant Jackson led that went something like this: "I may be poor."

Then everyone would respond, "I may be poor." Many who mouthed the words no doubt were.

"I may be without work."

"I may be without work," the people repeated.

"I may be hungry or sick."

"I may be hungry or sick." And one after another the various classifications were called.

Then Jackson would end. "But I am . . ."

And the people would shout back, "But I am . . ."

"Somebody,"

"Somebody," the shouting would continue.
"I am . . ."
"I am . . ."
"God's child."
"God's child."
What a great way to affirm truth, I remember thinking, *to hear about the dignity of all men from one's own lips.* Not all these people were believers, but it was nevertheless true that each one of them bore the mark of the Creator. Each one was a human being fashioned by his hand.

Everyone of these people needed to be reminded of this highly important truth. Though facing overwhelming problems, each one was still of great worth. None of them were alive because of accident or chance. Each person was a product of God's creative genius, and therefore a being of infinite value.

Perhaps you need to be reminded of the dignity you bear because of your Creator's original intent. Do you believe that? You may feel that because of age or sickness or circumstances or sin, your status in life is not too exciting. But the Scriptures state otherwise.

I want you to imagine a massive sheet of paper. At one extreme end, poke a pinhole. That will represent the earth.

Five-eighths of an inch away put a speck, the moon. Now travel nineteen feet from the pinhole, and cut a two-inch circle to stand for the sun. Mars will be twenty-nine feet, and Neptune is six hundred feet from the sun.

How far on your sheet of paper do you think you'll have to go in order to cut out the nearest star? Over one thousand miles from the pinhole! That's approximately the distance from Chicago to Denver.

Astronomers measure such vast distances in light years. That's the amount of space light covers in the course of a calendar year traveling at about one-hundred eighty-six thousand miles per second. In twelve months, the distance amounts to about 6 trillion miles, which doesn't mean anything because it's just too massive to comprehend.

Look at it this way. A bullet shot at the speed of light would circle the earth and hit you seven times before you could fall to the ground—even if it took just one second to fall.

Or if you were to travel at the speed of light, you could fly from Los Angeles to New York in one-sixtieth of a second. You would pass the moon one-and three-sixteenths seconds later, arrive at the sun in eight minutes, and cover our entire solar system in eleven hours. That nearest star would be reached in four-and three-tenths years. You would not arrive at the North Star until 400 years had passed! Crossing our galaxy, the Milky Way, would take one-hundred thousand years. And it's estimated outer space contains over one-hundred million galaxies like our Milky Way, each containing billions of stars. Little wonder the astronomy texts tell us that in the universe there are more heavenly bodies the size of our planet or larger than there are grains of sand upon the face of the earth.

Overwhelmed? Then you can identify with David who writes in Psalm 8, "When I look at thy heavens, the work of thy fingers, the moon and stars which thou hast established; what is man that thou art mindful of him, and the son of man that thou dost care for him?" (vv. 3, 4).

But the psalmist doesn't stop there. "Yet," he continues, "Thou hast made him little less than God, and dost crown him with glory and honor. Thou has given him dominion over the works of thy hands; thou hast put all things under his feet, all sheep and oxen, and also the beasts of the field, the birds of the air, and the fish of the sea, whatever passes along the paths of the sea" (vv. 5-8).

What David is saying is this. "When I consider the wonders of the heavens, I feel as though human beings are nothing. But this is not true. Why, God, you've crowned us with glory and honor. You have made man the very pinnacle of creation. In fact, we're just a little lower than heavenly beings."

David's contention is not that man is nothing but rather that he's wonderful! The great God who spoke into existence countless galaxies also decreed humans to be creatures of unique importance on this planet.

Such facts filled David's heart with praise. That's how Psalm 8 begins and ends. The opening and closing verses are the same. "O Lord, our Lord, how majestic is thy name in all the earth!" David glories in both who God is and what the Lord has made him to be.

There is something not only right, but also very thrilling about all this. In fact, to maintain any other attitude would be tragically wrong.

Let me illustrate. My father is a respected and successful businessman. Time and again he has gone out of his way to demonstrate his love for me, and most of the advantages I've been given in life, he's had a hand in. It's natural for me to be pleased in who my dad is and in what he has wanted for me as his child. If I were to be ashamed of him or apologetic for my background and what it has helped me to become, it would not only reflect badly on me but be a painful affront to him as well. Dad deserves the honor I give him, and I appreciate the advantages of being his offspring.

Should I be any less grateful for my relationship to my Heavenly Father? Of course not. To an even greater degree, I rejoice in who God is and in his intentions for me.

We humans have fallen far short of the potential God conferred on us at creation. But that doesn't mean God values us any less. Why, he went so far as to send his Son to Calvary to convince us of how strong his love is.

We fail to honor God when we say, "I'm a nobody." Or when we act as though he doesn't love us. Or when we fail to identify with him as our Father by following the imposter. These are almost unforgivable acts when we are God's children.

In a sentence, then, I'm affirming: *Glory is due God for the dignity he has bestowed on us.* Our lives should proclaim by words and actions to everyone we meet the greatness and the splendor and the worthiness of God. This certainly isn't going to be accomplished if we consistently go around discouraged, negative, and even sour on life.

"I can't help it," you say. "That's how I normally feel."

Are you open to an experiment? It's not hard. But prepare yourself not to instantly resist what I recommend. Sometimes I get the feeling certain people start shaking their heads, uh-huh, before I even make a suggestion! Instead start nodding your head up and down and thinking, "I bet this is going to be a great idea!"

Some night very soon I want you to spend a half hour outside looking at the stars. You may even want to take a slow walk down the street or meander through a park. Or you may prefer to just sit in the backyard and gaze at the heavens. If you're in the city, it's hard to see the stars because of artificial lights. But it's not that impossible.

I want you to invest thirty minutes viewing the stars. Are some especially beautiful to you? Figure out which celestial bodies are nearer and which ones are farther away. How long do you suppose they have been there? How many coming generations will enjoy this same view?

Start counting how many stars you can see. Who keeps them in such perfect order night after night? If an expert astronomer were available, which question would you ask?

Do you think the evening David wrote his psalm was something like the one you're experiencing? As the night progresses, do you think you might find it in your heart to say, as he did, "O Lord, how majestic is thy name in all the earth! I praise you for this spectacular evidence of your handiwork!"?

"I'll do it," you say.

Wait a minute, I'm not finished yet. Afterward, go inside and read Psalm 8 again. The only part I haven't covered is verse 2, which is the text Christ quotes while teaching in the temple after his triumphal entry. "Thou whose glory above the heavens is chanted by the mouth of babes and infants, . . . (Matt. 21:16).

I want you to especially notice the high position afforded mankind in this psalm. Verse 5 says that this same God who dotted the heavens with light crowned us with glory and honor—making us only a little lower than himself! Then, in quiet prayer, see if you can also give God the glory due him for the dignity he has bestowed on man.

2

THE OUTCOME OF WICKEDNESS:
Psalm 7

The focus of our interest in this chapter will be the wicked, or more specifically, those who conceive evil or mischief against others.

I've used those words because they appear in Psalm 7, which is my basic text. The writer is David and he is crying out for deliverance:

"O Lord my God, in thee do I take refuge; save me from all my pursuers and deliver me, lest like a lion, they rend me dragging me away, with none to rescue" (Ps. 7:1, 2).

Have you ever felt that way? I have! Read verse 9: "O let the evil of the wicked come to an end, but establish thou the righteous, thou who triest the minds and hearts, thou righteous God."

Of course, the big question is whether or not the Lord will indeed bring the evil of the wicked to an end, will he cause the lying and the violence to cease? That question is at the heart of this psalm.

David stated the matter in verses 14-16: "Behold, the wicked man conceives evil, and is pregnant with mischief, and brings forth lies. He makes a pit, digging it out, and falls into the hole which he has made. His mischief returns upon his own head, and on his own pate his violence descends."

This same thought is repeated in Psalm 9, verses 15 and 16, only then it's in the context of countries: "The nations have sunk in the pit which they made; in the net which they hid has their own foot been caught. The LORD has made himself known; he has executed judgment. . . . In the work of their own hands the wicked are snared."

Psalm 10 turns the idea into a prayer: "Why dost thou stand afar off, O LORD? Why dost thou hide thyself in times of trouble? In arrogance the wicked hotly pursues the poor; let them be caught in the schemes which they have devised."

Now the fact that specific sins do return to haunt the ones committing them is easily demonstrated from Scripture. For example, Adam and Eve refused to believe their Heavenly Father regarding right and wrong, only to have their children disobey them. At Babel, people planned to make a great name for themselves, but instead, they were unable to even understand the names of one another with the confusing of the languages.

As a young man, and with help from a little goat, Jacob tricked his aging father, Isaac, and he received the blessing that should have gone to his more favored older brother. But years later, Jacob's sons fooled him also by killing a little goat, cheating the favorite son out of what this aged father was planning to give him. Joseph's brothers find themselves in a reversed position, when they are unaware that Pharaoh's assistant, the man who holds their lives in his hand, is their brother Joseph.

It's kind of eerie, isn't it? Haman, who hanged from the gallows he built for Mordecai, is another illustration in Scripture of this principle of divine justice.

D. L. Moody told of a certain French king who wanted some new instruments with which to torture his prisoners. A favorite adviser suggested that he build a cage not long enough for a man to lie down and not high enough to stand up in. The monarch accepted the suggestion, but the first one put into the cage was the very man who had suggested it. He was kept in the device for fourteen years.

"But all your illustrations are unusual," you protest. "They are the exception and not the rule. Think how few times what you're saying is really true."

Granted, what I have to say might sound extreme. But I contend that this boomerang effect takes place far more often than we realize. Rather than force you to agree with me, however, I just suggest you begin to observe life more closely to see if it is not so. I've been doing this for some years now, so maybe that's why I am convinced the phenomenon occurs far more often than most of us suspect.

The consistent liar must now suffer being consistently lied about. The violent are served more than their share of physical abuse. The exploiter is exploited. The gossiper becomes the victim of loose and unkind tongues. The promiscuous taste the bitterness of another's promiscuity. The unsubmissive find great pain in leadership when their turn comes, because people under them refuse to submit. And on and on.

No, I cannot guarantee every misdeed will be rewarded exactly by the script, but I've seen retribution for evil come often enough to be fairly sure about it. In fact, I more or less just count on its taking place in time. *You can expect evil to return upon the head of the wicked*.

"If you persist in what you're doing," I told two men at my dining room table, "you will be the next ones to know the pain of what you're calling forth." It must have seemed improbable at the time. And who did I think I was to speak so boldly? They even shared my remark with others, who in turn shook their heads in disbelief. But less than two years later, I know they had different thoughts about my prophetic insight.

So much do I anticipate evil returning like an echo into the face of mischief makers that I frankly am afraid to pray like David does:

> 17He loved to curse; let curses come on
> him!
> He did not like blessing; may it
> be far from him!
> 18He clothed himself with cursings as
> his coat,
> may it soak into his body like
> water,
> like oil into his bones!

19May it be like a garment which he
    wraps around him,
like a belt with which he daily
    girds himself! . . .
29May my accusers be clothed with
    dishonor;
may they be wrapped in their own
    shame as in a mantle! (Ps. 109).

Such praying scares me because the likelihood of
these requests being granted is too great in my mind.
How would I feel when that happened?

David, who took another man's wife and later
suffered the sexual abuse of his own concubines, did
not hesitate to condemn his accusers.

6Appoint a wicked man against him;
    let an accuser bring him to trial.
7When he is tried, let him come forth
    guilty;
    let his prayer be counted as sin!
8May his days be few;
    may another seize his goods!
9May his children be fatherless,
    and his wife a widow!
10May his children wander about and
    beg;
    may they be driven out of the
    ruins they inhabit!
11May the creditor seize all that he
    has;
    may strangers plunder the fruits
    of his toil!

¹²Let there be none to extend kindness
     to him,
   nor any to pity his fatherless
     children!
¹³May his posterity be cut off;
   may his name be blotted out in
     the second generation!
¹⁴May the iniquity of his fathers be
     remembered before the LORD,
   and let not the sin of his mother be
     blotted out!
¹⁵Let them be before the LORD con-
     tinually;
   and may his memory be cut off
     from the earth ! (Ps. 109).

David had some pretty strong feelings about whoever it was that wronged him! Personally, I prefer to leave such matters in the hands of the Lord. "Vengeance is mine," he says in Romans 12:19. "I will repay." And quite often, I might add, it appears he does so in the same way the injustice was rendered.

But you say, "David, I'm still not convinced. There are just too many people getting by with more than they should to be satisfied with your simplistic observations." If that's your response, fine. I'm willing to let the matter rest for a while.

But first let me caution you: Because you see a person suffering a certain calamity, don't automatically assume he or she must have sometime pulled off a dirty trick that in one way or another resembles what that person is now having to bear. Remember also that all the returns on investments of wrongdoing don't necessarily have to be paid off during this lifetime.

Nevertheless, begin watching those who over a period of time trick and deceive people. See if through the years the Lord has not made sure they have received like measure. And if, as time passes, you become more and more convinced of what I'm sharing, you will have gained a valuable insight into life by expecting evil to return upon the head of the wicked.

Rather than being concerned about what seems to be a lack of justice being meted out to the ones who presently cause you pain, you will be more relaxed, knowing there will be a time of accounting before the supreme judge of the universe. We see just the foreshadowing of it now. But that's important as a symbolic down payment of what will some day be required.

You will also learn to be far more cautious about evil thoughts and actions against others, knowing what you sow is very likely what you will also reap.

I believe what I've shared is truth. I discovered it in God's Word. Just give it some time to prove itself on your behalf.

3

ADVICE FROM A MADMAN:
Psalm 34

The title for this chapter is a bit misleading. The writer of the psalm we'll examine really wasn't a madman. He just pretended to be.

If you are troubled, broken-hearted, crushed in spirit, ashamed, fearful or afflicted, you're among those who will profit most from these thoughts. That list isn't my compilation either. It comes right out of the text.

At the moment I don't personally identify with any of these descriptions, but I can clearly remember experiencing every one of these emotions at one time or another. Because of the pain I experienced, I'm conscious of not wanting to toss out words casually. I'm aware some of you are really hurting.

The situation of the writer was this: As a young man he had been praised nationally for his heroic deeds. At the same time he was forced to live like a hunted criminal because of the insane jealousy of his king.

"David?" you ask. That's right.

When we pick up David's story in 1 Samuel 21, we become familiar with the background for this chapter's main text: Psalm 34. Starting with 1 Samuel 21:10, the narrative reads:

> And David rose and fled that day from Saul, and went to Achish, the king of Gath. [Gath was the town from which Goliath hailed, the giant David had killed earlier.] And the servants of Achish said to him, "'Is not this David the king of the land? Did they not sing to one another of him in dances.
>
> 'Saul has slain his thousands, and David his ten thousands?'"
>
> And David took these words to heart, and was much afraid of Achish the king of Gath. So he changed his behavior before them, and feigned himself mad in their hands, and made marks on the doors of the gate, and let his spittle run down his beard (vv. 10-13).

If I were caught in a foreign city and such deception was my only way of escape, I think I'd have a hard time convincing anyone I was a genuine madman. It would take one incredible performance to pull off such a trick. Right?

But fearing for his life, David took the plunge and lo and behold, it worked! "Then said Achish to his servants, 'Lo, you see the man is mad; why then have you brought him to me? Do I lack madmen, that you have brought this fellow to play the madman in my house?'" (vv. 14, 15).

The next chapter begins, "David . . . escaped to the

cave of Adullam. . . . And every one who was in distress, and every one who was in debt, and every one who was discontented, gathered to him; and he became captain over them. And there were with him about four hundred men."

Reflecting on his close shave, but still not by any means out of the woods (or out of the caves), David wrote Psalm 34. Remember, however, he's still being hunted and is separated from his wife against his will. He's been cut off from Jonathan, his best friend and brother-in-law. The days of affliction and trouble, of fear and broken-heartedness, of being crushed in spirit and of feeling ashamed, have not yet ended. Remember this lest you assume the words of our psalm were written by someone who had it made.

In fact, I think this psalm sounds very much like something David might have taught the four hundred unfortunates who came to serve under him.

"Men, I have a new song. Sit down and listen to the words." Even though the incident isn't mentioned in the verses, the introduction to Psalm 34 reveals that this psalm was written when David feigned madness before the Philistine king at Gath.

¹I will bless the LORD at all
     times;
  his praise shall continually be in
     my mouth.
²My soul takes its boast in the LORD;
  let the afflicted hear and be glad.
³O magnify the LORD with me,
  and let us exalt his name together!

4 I sought the LORD, and he answered
　　me,
　and delivered me from all my fears.
5 Look to him, and be radiant;
　so your faces shall never be
　　ashamed.
6 This poor man cried, and the LORD
　　heard him,
　and saved him out of all his
　　troubles.
7 The angel of the LORD encamps
　around those who fear him, and
　　delivers them.
8 O taste and see that the LORD is good!
　Happy is the man who takes
　　refuge in him!
9 O fear the LORD, you his saints,
　for those who fear him have no
　　want!
10 The young lions suffer want and
　　hunger;
　but those who seek the LORD lack
　　no good thing.

11 Ccme, O sons, listen to me,
　I will teach you the fear of the
　　LORD.
12 What man is there who desires life,
　and covets many days, that he
　　may enjoy good?
13 Keep your tongue from evil,
　and your lips from speaking deceit.

14 Depart from evil, and do good;
    seek peace and pursue it.
15 The eyes of the LORD are toward
    the righteous,
    and his ears toward their cry.
16 The face of the LORD is against
    evildoers,
    to cut off the remembrance of
    them from the earth.
17 When the righteous cry for help,
    the LORD hears,
    and delivers them out of all their
    troubles.
18 The LORD is near to the broken-
    hearted,
    and saves the crushed in spirit.

19 Many are the afflictions of the
    righteous;
    but the LORD delivers him out of
    them all.
20 He keeps all his bones;
    not one of them is broken.
21 Evil shall slay the wicked;
    and those who hate the righteous
    will be condemned.
22 The LORD redeems the life of his
    servants;
    none of those who take refuge in
    him will be condemned.

"Aha, David!" "Very good, captain!" "Bravo!" "I like
it!" "Well done." "Sing it again." "Great!" Wouldn't it

have been satisfying to have been in the company of the four hundred when the psalm was first introduced?

Now the advice this pretend madman has given, reduced to a simple sentence, might sound something like this: *When in trouble, even unto death, the righteous should take refuge in God!*

By saying "take refuge in God," I believe David means we should turn to him for protection. Spend time in his presence. Tell him our needs. Meditate on his Word. Cry out to him for help. In short, make the Lord the focus of our trust.

In fact, I want to suggest some sections of Scripture that will be of help to anyone who is in a similar position. And I'll give a specific way to pray as well.

"Wait a minute!" someone shouts. "I'm in the pits, and you get my hopes up for some practical help. Now you're telling me the old line of 'read the Bible and pray.' What is this, anyway? I feel like I just got tricked instead of treated."

It's not my prerogative to change what David wrote. All I know is that he became mired in one mess after another, and yet the Psalms verify that he consistently brought these dilemmas before God—actually writing out his thoughts when he had time and "praying like mad" when he didn't.

Because it had worked for him, David could recommend the same to four hundred distressed, indebted, and discontented persons whose feelings were probably a lot like your own. "O taste and see that the Lord is good," he said. "Happy is the man who takes refuge in him! . . . The Lord redeems the life of his servants; none of those who take refuge in him will be condemned."

Granted, it's a song. Certainly it is not to be taken as a charm against harm of any kind. But I don't think you can beat what David has written. I for one agree with him. The best sanctuary to find when we are worried and upset and humiliated and struggling and broken-hearted is the Lord's presence. When in trouble, even unto death, the righteous should take refuge in God, said David.

You still feel shortchanged? Do you want to know what irritates me as a preacher? It's the number of Christians who go to everyone but the Lord for help when they're in trouble. Then they have the audacity to complain that he doesn't meet their needs! Could it be you're one of that group? I hope not!

Here are some additional helpful passages to read out loud and reflect on throughout the week. Psalms 3, 35, 86, and 142. Like Psalm 34, these are all David's songs. For additional reading of a narrative type, begin going through First and Second Samuel. You'll find all of these sections quite appropriate to your need, as is the Book of First Peter in the New Testament.

As for prayer, why not experiment with this format for a while. "Father, I want to talk with you about two things. The first is the problem I face. I want to explain that to you in detail. I also want to review out loud the qualities I know about you that might relate to my distressful situation."

To repeat, here is a prayer exercise for you. One, "God, here is the dilemma I face. I'm lonely and have never really been able to make friends . . . ;" two, "I believe you can help me because you are wise, and you are also truthful. I bring that attribute up because in

Psalm 34 you say to me, 'When the righteous cry for help, the Lord hears!' Then I'm confident you love me. . . !" Got it?

What you're saying is, "Here's the problem, Father. But I want to balance that viewpoint with an equally important review of the good qualities I know about you."

Advice from a madman? Hardly. More likely, it's a word from the Lord!

4

HURT BY A FRIEND:
Psalm 55

I'm wondering if you've ever experienced the intense
pain of being betrayed by someone close to you. I use
that word *betrayed* because I'm talking about something deeper than a temporary affront.

This person who was close to you has actually done
you serious wrong. Once you were intimate friends,
but not anymore, because he or she chose to undermine your position or reputation or character. The
breach may have been quite recent, but even if the
wound occurred years back, I imagine on occasion the
pain returns afresh.

Now I suspect a large percentage of us fit into this
"Yes—I've-been-hurt-badly-by-a-friend" category. I know
I do. The rift wasn't by my choice, nor have I encouraged
the separation. But I doubt strongly if the former relationship will ever return to what it once was.

Next weekend I have tickets for a production of Shakespeare's *Julius Caesar*. Shakespeare is a kind of hobby with our family. When the conspirators in the play, including Caesar's friend Brutus, stab the emperor and he pitifully cries, "Et tu, Brute! Then fall Caesar!" my stomach kind of turns. That knife from a friend is just too close to home. I'm sure many readers would feel the same way.

Could I interest you in some advice from a man who underwent similar treatment? David, the great king of Israel.

Ahithophel was his counselor. "In those days," says the Bible, "the counsel which Ahithophel gave was as if one consulted the oracle of God; so was all the counsel of Ahithophel esteemed, both by David and by Absalom." David, of course, was the king of Israel and Absalom was his third son. No one in Israel was as handsome, or so highly praised, it's recorded. From the sole of his foot to the crown of his head there was no defect in him.

Ambition and murder, however, dwelt inside Absalom. During his father's extreme displeasure over his vengeance killing, Absalom secretly began to plot to take over the throne. Part of his plan was to send for Ahithophel, David's famed counselor. Surprisingly, he, too, became involved in the scheming. The conspiracy grew strong, and the people with Absalom kept increasing, states the Scriptures. Hearing what was happening and caught unprepared, David fled Jerusalem.

Now let me read from 2 Samuel 15:30-31. "But David went up the ascent of the Mount of Olives, weeping as he went, barefoot and with his head covered, and all the people who were with him covered their heads. . . . And it was told David, 'Ahithophel is among the conspirators with Absalom.'"

Now, why had this man turned against his sovereign? We don't know for certain, but it seems a case can be built that he was the grandfather of Bathsheba. You remember her as the married woman with whom David had committed adultery some years earlier. Granted, such identity rests on whether or not Eliam, the son of Ahithophel, is the same man as the Eliam listed elsewhere as the father of Bathsheba. If he was, a motive is thus established for Ahithophel's actions. Anyway, it's interesting that upon entering Jerusalem, Absalom, on the advice of Ahithophel, publicly violated all David's harem.

Next listen to chapter 17 of 2 Samuel, from the first paragraph: "Moreover Ahithophel said to Absalom, 'Let me choose twelve thousand men, and I will set out and pursue David tonight. I will come upon him while he is weary and discouraged, and throw him into a panic; and all the people who are with him will flee; I will strike down the king only: . . . You seek the life of only one man, and all the people will be at peace.' And the advice pleased Absalom and all the elders of Israel." You'll have to read for yourself how the account ends.

This story is the setting for Psalm 55. Written by David before the matter had been resolved, it's about being knifed in the back by a friend and it reads as follows:

¹Give ear to my prayer, O God;
    and hide not thyself from my
        supplication!
²Attend to me, and answer me;

I am overcome by my trouble.
I am distraught [3] by the noise of the
    enemy,
   because of the oppression of the
    wicked.
For they bring trouble upon me,
   and in anger they cherish enmity
    against me.

[4] My heart is in anguish within me,
   the terrors of death have fallen
    upon me.
[5] Fear and trembling come upon me,
   and horror overwhelms me.
[6] And I say, "O, that I had wings like
    a dove!
I would fly away and be at rest;
[7] yea, I would wander afar,
   I would lodge in the wilderness,

[8] I would haste to find me a shelter
   from the raging wind and tem-
    pest."

[9] Destroy their plans, O Lord, confuse
    their tongues;
   for I see violence and strife in the
    city.
[10] Day and night they go around it
   on its walls;
and mischief and trouble are within
    it,
    [11] ruin is in its midst;

oppression and fraud
>do not depart from its market
>>place.

Now he becomes specific:

>¹²It is not an enemy who taunts me—
>>then I could bear it;
>it is not an adversary who deals
>>insolently with me—
>>then I could hide from him.
>¹³But it is you, my equal,
>>my companion, my familiar friend.
>¹⁴We used to hold sweet converse to-
>>gether;
>>within God's house we walked in
>>fellowship.
>¹⁵Let death come upon them;
>>let them go down to Sheol alive;
>>let them go away in terror into
>>their graves.

>¹⁶But I call upon God;
>>and the Lord will save me.
>¹⁷Evening and morning and at noon
>>I utter my complaint and moan,
>>and he will hear my voice.
>¹⁸He will deliver my soul in safety
>>from the battle that I wage,
>>for many are arrayed against me.
>¹⁹God will give ear, and humble them,
>>he who is enthroned from of old;
>because they keep no law,
>>and do not fear God.

20 My companion stretched out his
        hand against his friends,
    he violated his covenant.
21 His speech was smoother than butter,
        yet war was in his heart;
    his words were softer than oil,
        yet they were drawn swords.

And now in closing, David gives himself and his
readers advice:

22 Cast your burden on the LORD,
        and he will sustain you;
    he will never permit
        the righteous to be moved.

23 But thou, O God, wilt cast them down
        into the lowest pit;
    men of blood and treachery
        shall not live out half their days.
    But I will trust in Thee.

Well, that's Psalm 55. I hope from now on when you
read it, you'll always remember the historic context.
David was not manufacturing a solution to a problem
about which he knew nothing. No, he penned his words
in the pain of a real experience. And he came to the
conclusion that such burdens must be cast upon the
Lord. That's exactly what he's doing in this psalm. It's
the same advice he gave those four hundred men years
before in Psalm 34.

"That's right," you say, "one certainly needs to take
such problems to God!"

However, do you realize most people in such dilemmas do not think of doing this?

Some years ago, when my spirits were shattered because one of my most intimate friends sought to malign me, I remember how conversations with others left me feeling totally unfulfilled. Either they didn't understand what had happened, or I felt guilty even talking about the dark side of this man's character. Some people chatted about the situation academically, without empathizing with the awful heartbreak I bore.

It was different when I cried out to God. I knew he understood perfectly, because he had seen firsthand everything that had transpired. And in those many times alone together, his gentle spirit made me sensitive when I overstated my side or lost my objectivity.

It meant a great deal to me to know that my Lord had been betrayed by the kiss of a friend. In fact, some people say Psalm 55 describes Judas in the verses that begin, "My companion stretched out his hand against his friends, he violated his covenant . . ."

If you're struggling with similar feelings, I can tell you how helpful it was for me to be able to continually talk with the Lord. In fact, without this prayer outlet—this being able to cry out to God for a period of weeks and months ("in the morning, at noon, and in the evenings") —I don't know if I could have made it through that extended trial without cracking.

So, my words to you are not just a pat formula; they come out of the fire and parallel what the psalmist is saying: *Those betrayed by a friend should cast their burden on the Lord.*

In fact, I think it would be a great idea for those who feel betrayed to write out a prayer as David did.

Compose an on-the-spot psalm, if you please. Put on paper your feelings and what you're requesting of the Lord. It would be a great way to emulate the wise actions of one of the faith heroes of times past. It could also offer peace in the midst of the storm.

But will you do it? Or will you continue to believe relief is spelled in some other way?

> On God alone my soul relies,
> And He will soon relieve.
> The Lord will hear my plaintive cries,
> At morning, noon, and eve.
>
> Upon the Lord thy burden cast,
> To Him bring all thy care;
> He will sustain and hold thee fast,
> And give thee strength to bear.

5

PRAYER FOR A SON:
Psalm 72

Have you ever been thanked for somthing you didn't
do? On occasion people have told me how a certain
radio message of mine changed their entire life, when
actually it was one that John D. Jess, the founder of our
broadcast, had preached. People have even informed
me of helpful advice I gave them, which they followed to
the letter, and everything turned out just great. But
apparently they misunderstood. Because if I remember
correctly, what I said was exactly the opposite of what
they thought they heard!

All of which sets up a similar experience in my own
study in the Psalms. When I first read Psalm 72, I took it
to be King David's prayer on behalf of his son and not
too distant successor, Solomon. Here's how it begins:

¹Give the king thy justice, O
    God,

and thy righteousness to the royal
son!
2 May he judge thy people with righteousness,
and thy poor with justice!
3 Let the mountains bear prosperity
for the people,
and the hills, in righteousness!
4 May he defend the cause of the poor
of the people,
give deliverance to the needy,
and crush the oppressor!

That's the first four of the twenty verses.
Isn't that great, I thought, *here's a prayer of a father
for his son. What a beautiful picture.* I read further:

9 May his foes bow down before him,
and his enemies lick the dust!
10 May the kings of Tarshish and of the
isles
render him tribute,
May the kings of Sheba and Seba
bring gifts!
11 May all the kings fall down before him,
all nations serve him!

12 For he delivers the needy when he
calls,
the poor and him who has no
helper.

Now I pray regularly for my children, but I've never
written a prayer of intercession like this on their behalf. *I*

must do that sometime, I thought, and continued investigating what David asked for Solomon.

¹⁵May prayer be made for him con-
    tinually,
  and blessings invoked for him all
    the day!
¹⁶May there be abundance of grain in
    the land;
  on the tops of mountains may
    it wave;
  may its fruit be like Lebanon;
and may men blossom forth from the
    cities
  like the grass of the field!

Then verse 20 concludes: " The prayers of David, the son of Jesse, are ended."

Well, the experience of writing out extended prayers for my children has proven to be so profitable to me personally I decided to write a chapter about it.

That's when the surprise came! Doing research to augment my private reading, I discovered that many scholars don't think David wrote this psalm! They say it belongs to the group of Messianic Psalms, psalms about the coming Messiah. Solomon is not the subject, and the title "A Psalm to Solomon," or "For Solomon" in some Bibles, reads "A Psalm *of* Solomon" in others. So, the prayer of King David for his son, the future ruler, suddenly began to vanish before my eyes.

I studied it again. Some of the words did go beyond the scope of a human ruler. Verses 7 and 8: "In his day may righteousness flourish, and peace abound, *till the moon be no more!* May he have dominion from sea to sea, and from the River to the ends of the earth!"

Or verse 17: "May his name endure for ever, his fame continue as long as the sun! May men bless themselves by him, all nations call him blessed!" Yes, I could see why some interpreters felt the passage referred to someone greater than Solomon.

In fact, this psalm has served as the basis for some of our greatest hymns about Christ, like that one of Isaac Watts:

Jesus shall reign where'er the sun
does his successive journeys run;
His kingdom spread from shore to shore,
Till moons shall wax and wane no more.
To Him shall endless prayer be made,
And endless praises crown His head;
His name like sweet perfume shall rise
With every morning sacrifice."

The thoughts come right out of the text.
Or the one by James Montgomery:

Hail to the Lord's Anointed,
Great David's greater son!
Hail, in the time appointed,
His reign on earth begun!
He comes to break oppression,
To set the captive free,
To take away transgression
And rule in equity.

There is a helpful footnote in the Jerusalem Bible that reads: "This Psalm, dedicated to Solomon whose wealth, glory and just and peaceful reign it celebrates, evokes the image of the future ideal king. Jewish and Christian traditions see it as a portrait of the messianic king, foretold by Isaiah and Zachariah." These two sentences put the mystery into perspective.

What was written in Psalm 72 has a definite historic setting. But like Psalm 22, where David cries out, "They pierced my hands and feet, . . . they divide my garments among them, and for my raiment they cast lots," the words transcend the immediate situation and relate in a most unusual way to the Messiah himself.

So it might not be appropriate for me to thank David for establishing the precedent of writing a prayer for his children. But the exercise proved so helpful that I want to tell you what I discovered. And, of course, it's quite possible this really is a psalm David first wrote for his son, Solomon. But the guidance of the Holy Spirit also gave it Messianic overtones.

When you start to write a prayer for one of your children, I think you'll find, as I did, that you're suddenly in a different frame of mind than when you simply talk to the Lord about one of them. Spoken prayers tend to relate to the immediate. They center on today, tomorrow, and next week, or maybe the school year.

But when you actually take paper and pen in hand and begin to think of what you're going to write down, you take a long-range view. The fact that your words will remain changes your perspective.

Knowing I won't be here forever, how shall I pray for, say, my six year old? "Well, Father, I want his walk with you to continue, so I pray for all those who will touch him spiritually through the years. Please give his Sunday school teachers, pastors, camp counselors, and, of course, relatives, a special love for this boy. He could be overlooked, but because of my prayers I shall expect people to see him through the eyes of Christ.

"Because I want my son to enjoy the beauty and magnificence and good of this great world you have made, I pray you will ordain his schooldays so that he has the finest teachers available. Conversely, protect him from those who sow anti-God thoughts. Because you oversee his life, may he also be exposed to what is truly the best of human giftedness in order to stimulate his own creativity. At the same time, I ask that unnecessary evil be eliminated.

"May the essentials of food and clothing and shelter become secondary concerns as he learns to seek your kingdom first. And, if possible, I pray for peace during his lifetime."

Well, this is an entirely different prayer than I would normally make for a child. An additional benefit from writing out what I really want for each of my four children is that I feel greatly aided in my regular prayers for them.

For my oldest, a fifteen year old, the exercise assumes different dimensions. I pray for the unknown girl he may someday marry. But then I also ask that he will be open to being single for the sake of the Kingdom if that is God's will. Because our eldest can understand more of the faith than his younger brother, I also ask that Randy will develop a high sensitivity to the promptings of the Holy Spirit. "Also, Father, begin to instill in him now a great hunger for your Word."

Well, you get the idea.

"I sure do," you say. "But my children are grown and married, mister, so it's a little late to be thinking of future marriage partners and so on!"

It wasn't too late for David. I'm sure Solomon was a grown man when Psalm 72 was penned. Besides, do parents stop praying for their children when they become adult? I hope mine haven't!

In a sentence then, here's what I'm saying: *It is good to write a prayer for a son or a daughter.* It is good to put on paper your deepest feelings regarding each child and what you want God to do.

Now it's not important that what you draft be poetic or artistic, but rather that you truly express to God your strongest desires for your infant or child or youth or early adult, even that mature member of society. The beauty is, of course, that God hears and answers prayer.

Why not get paper and jot down some of your initial thoughts right now?

6

REJOICING IN EACH DAY:
Psalm 118

Which of the following two characterizations best describes the kind of person you are?

One: Normally you don't particularly notice things like sunsets or birds singing or the stars coming out at night. When you travel the scenery just passes by.

Two: You relish the arrival of flowers in the spring; you see beauty in a fresh blanket of snow. You even enjoy walking in a light drizzle.

Did you identify with one of these descriptions? Let me attempt several other contrasts. How do you wake up in the morning? Grudgingly, reluctantly, not really sure you want to rejoin the human race for another go at things? Or do you awaken with a glad heart, happy to be alive, and grateful for another day and the opportunities it affords?

What about eating? Are you among those who hardly

recognize the taste of what's been served because your mind is elsewhere? Are meals strictly a secondary function, wasted time unless you can talk with a client or read a paper? Or do you think mealtimes are important in themselves? If necessary, you take the phone off the hook during supper so the family, without interruption or hurry, can enjoy one another and what has been lovingly prepared.

What about Sunday mornings? Do you resent having to get ready for church, sometimes feeling jealous of your neighbor who's still sleeping as you pull out of the drive with nothing but a fast cup of coffee to keep you until noon? Or do you look to the Lord's Day as the high point of your week, the best of all days, the time to meet with fellow believers in God's house, joining voices together in praise? Is Sunday so important to you that you begin getting ready for it on Saturday evening through prayer and a good night's sleep?

Well, I can't say into which group *you* fit, but I do know that the God who made us intended for human beings to find joy in his world and himself as well. The old catechisms say the chief end of man is to love God and enjoy him forever.

Yet, in our over-busy, highly competitive, man-centered world, I question whether most people have retained the simple joy of rising in the morning and looking forward with pleasure to a new day. Too many, I fear, have little or no appreciation for the beauty of the home God fashioned for his earthlings. They live with almost no conscious sense of his immanence.

In direct contrast to this negative attitude are the words of Psalm 118:24: "This is the day which the Lord has made; let us rejoice and be glad in it."

"Ah, that sounds like another one of King David's spiritual saccharine pills," I can almost hear someone say. "If I were a handsome king who was praised by everyone, had a houseful of servants, unlimited finances, and all the spouses I wanted, I'd probably look forward to getting up in the morning, too."

Well, wait just a minute! This is not one of David's psalms. Psalm 118 was written after Israel's exile in Babylon, and it was probably sung at the dedication of the new temple. It was certainly used on some such occasion. And the text is not without reference to hardships (vv. 5-7): "Out of my distress I called on the LORD; the LORD answered me and set me free. . . . The LORD is on my side to help me; I shall look in triumph on those who hate me."

Even more sobering is the fact that scholars believe this is the psalm Christ sang with the disciples at the Passover feast (Matt. 26). You remember it reads, "and when they had sung a hymn, they went out to the Mount of Olives (Matt 26:30).

The truth is, you ought to read through Psalm 118 several times. First, see it through the eyes of those present when the rebuilt temple was officially dedicated. Imagine the excitement as the great multitude of returned exiles sang, "Open to me the gates of righteousness, that I may enter through them and give thanks to the Lord" (v. 19).

Then read Psalm 118 a second time, thinking of what it would have meant to Jesus as he sang these words in the upper room on that last night he lived. Take verse 26, for instance. Remember what the people cried earlier in the week as he entered Jerusalem on a donkey? "Blessed is he who comes in the name of the Lord!" (Matt. 21:9).

What emotion did Christ feel when he sang verse 6 with the twelve: "With the Lord on my side I do not fear. What can man do to me?"

Or verse 17: "I shall not die, but I shall live, and recount the deeds of the Lord."

Or look at verse 22: "The stone which the builders rejected has become the chief cornerstone." And verse 24: "This is the day which the Lord has made: let us rejoice and be glad in it."

Finally, read through the psalm for yourself, recognizing that these are not naive, simplistic thoughts, but eternal words from God.

Concentrate on the text I've chosen, verse 24. It says: "Let us rejoice (in this day) and be glad in it." In other words, let us anticipate God's divine providence over all that transpires today. As these hours unfold, may we experience his closeness and delight in his goodness. May our mindset be to celebrate the fact that God is alive and active in our world.

This attitude is in striking contrast to those who are apparently oblivious to the ever-present touch of God in their lives. Worse yet are those who complain in spiritual blindness. His overwhelming care would be very obvious if their eyes were open. But unfortunately they live on the premise that they are on their own. God does not enter into their thoughts.

Since Psalm 118 was the favorite of Martin Luther, let me retell an oft-repeated story. His wife, Katie, tired of one of Martin's extended periods of depression, appeared dressed in black.

"How come?" he asked her.

"Oh, I'm mourning a death," she replied.

"Whose?"

"God's"

"God's not dead."

"Oh, really now? The way you've been acting of late I figured he must be. Certainly it appears as if he no longer cares for you."

Her point was well made.

We can laugh at this domestic drama from the past, but what has been your attitude of late? Do you manifest an appreciation of God in your life? Or can the day pass without once being consciously aware that he is very good to his children? The psalmist says that each new morning brings the privilege of again experiencing the marvelous hand of God on a life. And I'm just repeating his message. In a sentence, I'm putting it like this: *God intends that his people rejoice in the privilege of each new day.*

Granted, some reading these words are in travail, even as Christ was when he sang them that evening before he died. In your case, I'll let the Lord apply his words to you as he desires.

For the many who have no real cause to weep, but for some reason seem unable to rejoice in the fact that God is alive and active in your world, let me suggest the following:

First, starting now, begin a thank-you notebook by writing down ten items for which you are grateful to the Lord. Put another ten down tomorrow—and more if you want to, but never less than ten. I will guarantee that before the week is over you'll be surprised at how much more conscious you are of the Lord's goodness toward you. The second week you'll probably feel ashamed about all you previously took for granted.

By the end of the month you'll be noting not only answers to prayer, but the many good gifts of life— health and a job and freedom and a church home and friends and beautiful children. Before long you'll begin to see beauty in the world around you: the pair of Canada geese that flew overhead so gracefully, the neighbor's litter of cute new puppies, the breeze that felt so good when it came, the needed rain.

Second, when praying before a meal, give thanks by name for each item you'll be eating. Tell the Lord what you like about what you've been served. Food is one of God's gifts to men. Why gulp it down like the family dog and not even remember what you've swallowed?

Third, first thing up in the morning, tell the Lord, "Because you expect me to rejoice in this day, I will." Say it right now: "God, because you intend that I rejoice in this day, I will." Write the sentence on a paper and place it by the bed so you will read it when you wake. "God, because you intend that I rejoice in this day, I will."

Last, find a song that expresses this basic thought and sing it. "When morning gilds the skies my heart awakening cries; May Jesus Christ be praised." There's a new chorus, "Love him in the morning when you see the sun arising."

Join Reginald Heber in "Holy, Holy, Holy, Lord God Almighty! Early in the morning our song shall rise to Thee."

Try Harriet Beecher Stowe's hauntingly beautiful "Still, still with Thee, when purple morning breaketh, when the bird waketh and the shadows flee; fairer than morning, lovelier than the daylight, dawns the sweet consciousness, I am with thee."

That says it well, doesn't it? You get the idea. God intends for his people to rejoice in the privilege of each new day.

7

PROCRASTINATION:
Psalm 119

I might try to be funny and say, "I've been wanting to write on procrastination for some time now, but I've just kept putting it off."

That really wouldn't be true (and probably wouldn't be too humorous either). I do know that with the many things occupying people's time, procrastination continues to be a big problem in our society.

The word *procrastination* comes from the Latin, *pro*, meaning forward, plus *cras*, which is tomorrow. Hence it means "to put forward to tomorrow." The problem doubtless relates to any area you might name, but my concern is its effect on spiritual matters.

There is a story of imps and demons holding a conference to determine the best possible means of keeping people from responding to God's love. A panel of successful enemy workers had been asked to share the methods they found most successful in their fight for human souls.

"My approach has always been to undermine their belief in Scripture," boasted one. "It's a tremendous advantage to get people to feel these writings can't be trusted, and I do everything I can to bring them materials that promote such doubt!"

"I try to focus their attention on the shortcomings of anyone they know who has gone over to the Enemy," said another. "This is a natural, because earthlings don't want to believe someone else has become better than themselves. So I parade every flaw I can find—real or imagined. I've found this works in a great majority of the assignments I've been given."

Another idea was aired on the conference floor. "My most effective technique is to emphasize what a good *man* the Enemy's son was, but I oppose every mention of his deity. This gives what I'm doing the appearance of openness and fairness, and people really like that."

There were many ideas put forward, but the delegates really awaited the words of one who had not yet spoken. Everyone knew his success record was far and beyond that of any other demon. At last this seasoned veteran in the affairs of darkness raised his arm for silence.

"I have appreciated the reports of others. Now I offer advice from my personal experience. More and more I rely on a single approach. No longer do I try to undermine Scripture. When people read it, they somehow sense its truth.

"Nor do I point out the flaws of Christians. Sooner or later the beauty of their new life will begin to show, and then what? I even go so far as to agree that Jesus was the Messiah. He died and rose again to recapture men from the forces of the rebellion.

"Yes, I even agree that my target would be wise to respond to him. My great success has come from suggesting that he put it off a little. Tomorrow . . . do it tomorrow, do it tomorrow, do it tomorrow!' "

I wonder how many have fallen victim to such an approach? I think the enemy uses this ploy on believers as well as nonbelievers.

For example, as soon as a person becomes a Christian, Satan's henchmen change the approach slightly, but the aim is the same. "You know what? When you become more proficient in prayer, you really ought to . . ."

"When the children are more manageable you can . . ." Or "When you make just a little more money . . ."

"After you become involved in a church . . ." or "following your schooling . . ."

After this or that "when" comes, the tempter always has a new variation on the theme. So his victims go on imagining great victories that fail to materialize because their tomorrow never comes. Rather than attacking your good intentions the enemy agrees with them, all the while holding the dream in front of you like the crafty rider of a stupid donkey dangles a carrot on a string before his nose.

Read Psalm 119, verses 59 and 60: "When I think of thy ways, I turn my feet to thy testimonies; I hasten and do not delay to keep thy commandments."

Because the psalm begins by talking about who the blessed are—those happy, fortunate, to-be-envied people—I feel the following sentence fairly represents the text: *Blessed are those who pursue God's desires today!* Instead of dallying, they get about the business *now* of doing what they feel would please God.

Well, the sentence sounds good, but it will have minimal value unless we can nail it down with specifics. Blessed are people like you who pursue God's desires today—by reserving evenings for the study of Scripture, sharing your faith with a friend, conquering a troublesome sin, spending more quality time with your children, changing the way of handling your money, making things right with a brother or sister in the Lord. These are merely illustrations of how exacting we need to get.

If God were to speak to you right now about something that needed change, what would he name? Could you fill in the blank?

For some of you that's an easy question. One specific matter immediately pops into your mind. "He would say I should work on the relationship with my spouse." Or "I should stop talking about so-and-so the way I do."

For others, the question may be confusing, because you can think of a dozen possible things that might be his desire for you. Well, since working on any one of them would no doubt please God, those in this category only need to choose one.

Others might find the question requires time for reflection. If God were to name one area of concern in my life, what would it be? Perhaps you should stop your reading and ponder awhile.

It is crucial to target specific matters. Otherwise you may read my words and just feel dreadfully guilty. If you can experience success in one specific area, this may be all you really need in order to achieve momentum in all areas of your walk with God.

So when I ask, "What is your problem area?", be specific. Instead of naming procrastination, which is too general, say, "I fail to show an interest in my children's spiritual growth." Or "I don't take myself in tow regarding the amount of time I watch television." "I'm delaying becoming involved in any kind of service for Christ, even with the gifts he has given me." These are all specifics that can bring rejoicing when progress results.

Question number two: If today you *were* to spend a half hour in your Bible or if you made that apology you've been pretending wasn't necessary, *how do you think you would feel?* Maybe I can ask it this way. If you began to do what you sense God desires of you, would it make you happy or sad?

Isn't it strange! The enemy spreads the big lie that there is joy only on his side of the line. But it's not true! The person who does what God says is the one who is truly happy or fortunate or blessed or to be envied.

Knowing this, the psalmist writes, "I hasten and do not delay to keep thy commandments" (v. 60). Paraphrased this might read, "Having walked with God for some time and knowing firsthand how good he is, I rush to obey when he speaks." Maybe I should add a touch of acceleration to the key sentence: *Blessed are those WHO HASTEN TO pursue God's desires today!* Yes, that's even better!

Have you had a mental block regarding the spiritual matter that's been hanging over your head for so long? Well, if you would just start, you might be surprised how quickly it begins to dissolve. Usually the hardest part of growth is getting going. But there's nothing keeping you from doing that today, is there?

"David, do you really think your words are going to move anyone to change patterns that have been years in the making?"

Well, no; not *my* words, anyway. But I've been praying as I put this chapter together that God would use this truth taken from his word so many will see not just my thoughts but his as well. I've been in the ministry long enough to know that when this happens, the results can be amazing.

When prompted by a divine nudge, people have been known to break bad habits, start down the road of meaningful praying, restore injured relationships, conquer lust, change their pattern of irritability, become more responsible, tell the truth, love their neighbor, pay their bills, witness for the Lord, master Scripture, release themselves from self-pity. At your very age, some have even been led to change their allegiance from Satan to God.

Without exception, all who have responded to the divine nudge are glad they did, because blessed are those who hasten to pursue God's desires today.

In other words, blessed are those who do not put off what God desires by saying, "I'll do it tomorrow. I'll do it tomorrow . . . do it tomorrow . . . tomorrow."

8

FROM GENERATION TO GENERATION:
Psalm 145

How difficult it is to imagine living in a society where people who can read are in the minority and whatever reading material is available is not printed but copied by hand. But if you'll go in imagination back into the setting of the author whose writings we're studying, you'll need to eliminate radio, tv, postal services, and telephones. Learning is communicated through oral tradition. This will be the chief means of knowledge about both past and present as opposed to our modern utilization of newspapers, magazines, and books.

Historians feel, however, that this verbal system wasn't really all that bad. In ancient times, man learned to be proficient at retaining facts and saw to it that important information was correctly passed on through the years. So, apart from the written scrolls usually kept by the elite class of priests, elders met with townsfolk and fathers told their families about events. All this consistently tied the people to what was illustrious in terms of their past.

From such an era, then, King David's words in Psalm 145 are penned:

> 3 Great is the LORD, and greatly to be
> praised,
> and his greatness is unsearchable.

> 4 One generation shall laud thy works
> to another,
> and shall declare thy mighty acts.

> 7 They shall pour forth the fame of
> thy abundant goodness,
> and shall sing aloud of thy right-
> eousness.

> 11 They shall speak of the glory of thy
> kingdom,
> and tell of thy power,
> 12 to make known to the sons of men
> thy mighty deeds,
> and the glorious splendor of thy
> kingdom.
> 13 Thy kingdom is an everlasting king-
> dom,
> and thy dominion endures through-
> out all generations.

This lauding of God and his ways was to continue down the line from town leaders to people and from clan heads to family members. The intent of the psalm, however, is that the praise sharing was not to be limited only to accounts of God's past supernatural workings. Yes, praise him for what he did under the patriarchs and Moses and Samuel and Gideon and Samson. To forget such mercies would be tragic. But the psalm also says: "The Lord is near to all who call upon him, to all who call upon him in truth. He fulfills the desire of all who fear him, he also hears their cry, and saves them" (vv. 18-19).

There were to be expressions of gratitude and praise for divine benefits in the present time as well. Thus, this verbal rehearsing of what God was doing served as a continuing reminder of the important role played by God in the life of people from yesterday to today. The Lord was not distant, nor was he unconcerned about his own, but repetition of his historic care was important. In fact, this sharing can be seen as an early form of mass communication. If the system broke down, an important aspect of the spiritual life of the people was missed.

All of us are aware of Old Testament Israel's strange ability to fall away from God. If you realize, however, that each family was actually only a single generation away from ignorance regarding Jehovah, then you can see why this verbal passing of the baton of faith was necessary. To be effective it must continue unbroken.

How is our present generation doing in its job of passing on what is spiritually significant? Obviously, we are blessed with every means of communication one could imagine. Still, I wonder sometimes if people suffer from overkill. Without the constant bombardment of an information blitz, perhaps the population of earlier eras was better equipped to retain what was important.

At least, I'm quite sure that Israel had a better comprehension of the way God had worked in their nation than most believers of various countries do nowadays. For example, in the United States I find Christians almost illiterate when it comes to knowing about the special times of brightness, such as the Great Awakening when God worked mightily on our American soil. Unfortunately , I also fear key figures of that period, like Jonathan Edwards or George Whitefield, are not appreciated as they should be. Is it fair to equate this with Israel forgetting Joshua and Caleb?

Let me share with you a startling account I found the other day. It was written by a Connecticut farmer and gives a glimpse of what was happening in the colonies during that incredible period. The sentences are long (he's not a writer), but his words are extremely descriptive and authentic.

Now it pleased God to send Mr. Whitefield into this land and my hearing of his preaching at Philadelphia like one of the old apostles and many thousands flocking after him to hear the gospel and great numbers were converted to Christ, I felt the Spirit of God drawing me by conviction. I longed to see and hear him and wished he would come this way and I soon heard he was to come to New York and the Jersies and great multitudes flocking after him under great concern for their souls and many converted which brought on my concern more and more, hoping soon to see him but next I heard he was on Long Island and next at Boston and next at Northhampton, and then one morning all on a sudden about 8 or 9 o'clock, there came a messenger and said Mr. Whitefield preached at Hartford and Wethersfield yesterday and is to preach at Middletown this morning at 10 o'clock. I was in my field at work. I dropt my tool that I had in my hand and ran home and ran through my house and had my wife get ready quick to go and hear Mr. Whitefield preach at Middletown and ran to my pasture for my horse with all my might, fearing I should be too late to hear him. I brought my horse home and soon mounted and took my wife up and went forward as fast as I thought the horse could bear and when my horse began to be out of breath I would get down and put my wife on the saddle and bid her ride as fast as she could and not stop or slack for me except I bade her and so I would run until I was almost out of breath and then mount my horse again and so I did several times to favor my horse. We improved every moment to get along as if we were fleeing for our lives, all this while fearing we should be too late to hear the sermon for we had twelve miles to ride double in little more than an hour and we went round by the upper parish and when we came within half a mile of the road that comes down from Hartford, Wethersfield, and Stepney to Middletown on high land I saw before me a cloud or fog rising, I first thought off from the Great River, but as I came nearer the road I heard a noise something like a low, rumbling thunder and I presently found it was the rumbling of horses' feet coming down the road, and this cloud was a cloud of dust made by the running of horses feet, it arose some rods into the air over the tops of the hills and trees, and when I came within about twenty rods of the road I could see men and horses slipping along in the cloud like shadows and when I came nearer it was like a steady stream of horses, and their riders, scarcely a horse more than his length behind another, all of a lather and foam with sweat, their breath rolling out of their nostrils, in a cloud of dust every jump, every horse seemed to go with all his might to carry his rider to hear the news from Heaven to the saving of their souls. It made me tremble to see the sight how the world was in a struggle. I found a vacance between two horses to slip in my horse and my wife said, 'Law, our clothes will be all spoiled, see how they look'—for they were so covered with dust they looked almost all of a color, coats and hats and shirts and horses. We went down in the stream. I heard no man speak a word all the way, three miles, but everyone pressing forward in great haste and when we got down to the old meeting-house there was a great multitude, it was said to be 3 or 4000 of people assembled together. We got off from our horses and shook off the dust and the ministers was then coming to the meeting-house. I turned and looked toward the Great River and saw the ferry boats running swift forward and backward bringing over loads of people, the oars rowed nimble and quick; everthing, men, horses and boats seemed to be struggling for life; the land and the banks over the river looked black with people and horses. All along the twelve miles I see no man at work in his field but all seemed to be gone. When I see Mr. Whitefield come up upon the scaffold he looked almost angelical, a young slim slender youth before some thousands of people and with a bold undaunted countenance. And my hearing how God was with him everywhere as he came along it solemnized my mind and put me in a trembling fear before he began to preach for he looked as if he was clothed with authority from the great God and a sweet solemn solemnity sat upon his brow, and my hearing him preach gave me a heart wound and by God's blessing. . . . My old foundation was broken up and I saw my righteousness would not save me" (From *The Church of Our Fathers* by Roland H. Bainton [Scribner's, 1979], and *George Whitefield* by Arnold Dallimore [Good News, 1979]).

It's quite an account, isn't it? Yet, it's as though this heritage has been all but lost from the memory of most modern American Christians.

Historic illiteracy is certainly not what Psalm 145 is advocating. I also wonder if the lauding of God regarding what he's doing in the present is fresh with each new generation of believers. Do we insure continuity of belief by verbally rehearsing what is most important—the testimony of our walk with God? Among the countless words being spoken each day, is what he is doing receiving the emphasis it should? Do members of your household know the answers to questions such as, "Dad, mom, in your lifetime did God reveal himself in some special way? And what about you personally; can you share with me how he showed himself faithful on your behalf?"

Maybe the time has come to seriously consider what you have to contribute to the rehearsing of God's greatness from parent to child. A break in the chain is still tragic.

I thank God for people I know who have come to grips with this issue. "Yes, my kids have heard me talk about the business, sports, tv, cars, the whole bit . . . but not the Lord, and that's going to change," said one friend of mine. It did, and I'm proud of him. But there need to be many more, and maybe you're one of them.

Why? Well, because letting someone else do it probably won't impress your children. There is nothing to compare with the intimate testimony, day in and day out, of a life that they observe and know. Maybe it's still true that *each generation must continue the lauding of God's great works.*

May we all be like David who in the concluding verses of Psalm 145 says, "My mouth will speak the praise of the LORD, and let all flesh bless his holy name for ever and ever."